LIFE IN EXTREME ENVIRONMENTS™

LIFE IN THE DESERT

KATHERINE LAWRENCE

The Rosen Publishing Group, Inc., New York

For Elice James Coe, with thanks for twenty-two years of friendship, and a shared love of the Mojave and Sonoran Deserts

Published in 2004 by The Rosen Publishing Group, Inc.
29 East 21st Street, New York, NY 10010

Library of Congress Cataloging-in-Publication Data

Lawrence, Katherine.
Life in the desert/Katherine Lawrence.— 1st ed.
      p. cm.—(Life in extreme environments)
Summary: Defines the desert and indicates how plants, animals, and humans learn to survive in this extreme environment.
Includes bibliographical references (p. 57).
ISBN 0-8239-3985-5 (lib. bdg.)
1. Deserts—Juvenile literature. 2. Desert survival—Juvenile literature.
[1. Deserts. 2. Desert ecology. 3. Desert survival. 4. Ecology. 5. Survival.]
I. Title. II. Series.
QH88.L385 2003
577.54—dc21

2002156616

Manufactured in the United States of America

CONTENTS

INTRODUCTION: DESERTS AREN'T ALWAYS HOT

The sun beats down on your head and shoulders like the weight of your book bag on the worst homework day of the year. The air is so hot that every breath you take scorches your lungs. Your mouth is so dry that when you try to lick your lips you can't produce any saliva. All you feel is the pressure of your tongue, which makes the skin on your lips crack and split. You squint, but the light pours in through your eyelashes. It's the desert.

Then the sun goes down. The clear skies and dryness of the air cause the temperature to drop amazingly fast. By the time you can see the stars clearly, you're beginning to feel cool. By midnight, you're shivering and so cold that you'd better have blankets with you if you want to get any sleep. Though it may

The desert at night can be bitterly cold. Temperatures at Ayers Rock *(above)* at Uluru National Park in Australia can fall as low as -8 degrees Celsius (about 17 degrees Fahrenheit).

seem hard to believe, you're still in the desert. After all, what defines a desert isn't the extremely hot temperature, it's the lack of moisture. The proper definition of a desert is any ecosystem where a lack of available water places severe limits on living things.

Just how severe those limitations need to be for an area to be considered a desert is one of the things scientists have been arguing about for years. In general, according to David Wentworth Lazaroff in the *Arizona-Sonora Desert Museum*

Book of Answers, "Wherever much more moisture could theoretically be evaporated from the soil than is actually delivered by precipitation, a desert will result." Michael Allaby offers a simpler definition in *Biomes of the World, Volume 2: Deserts*: "A desert is likely to form if the average amount of precipitation is less than ten inches [250 millimeters] a year." (Compare this to the more than 40 inches [1,000 millimeters] of combined rain, snow, and ice in much of the United States and Canada.)

Despite these definitions, no two scientists seem to agree on just how many deserts there are. For example, some include the Arctic and Antarctica because there's so little available moisture; most of it is frozen into ice. There are so many variations in plant and animal life, elevation, temperature, and precipitation that it's impossible to give "just the facts" about deserts.

What is possible is to talk about what kind of place a desert is. What kinds of plants and animals live there? How and why do people live in such an extreme environment? And since there are five deserts within North America, what do you need to know if you're visiting the desert and get lost? What would it take to survive?

CHAPTER ONE

THE WEIRD, THE BIZARRE, AND THE DEADLY

Extremes in the desert aren't limited to dryness or temperature. The plants, animals, and insects of the desert are as extraordinary as their environment—and sometimes as deadly. Because there are so many desert dwellers and so much information available on the Web and in libraries, here are just a few of the highlights. (To see a chart of the major deserts in the world, see pages 34–38.)

THE WEIRD

Weird means the odd, the fantastic, the mysterious. While all biomes include plants and creatures that fit

These two-humped Bactrian camels are perfectly suited to the desert and semidesert regions of China. They are able to go without water for seven to ten days—even under a scorching sun—during which time they may lose between 22 and 25 percent of their total body weight. Unlike their wild cousins in the Gobi Desert, these Bactrian camels are put to work and provide wool, meat, and milk.

this description, deserts are filled with them. Listed here are some you might encounter in deserts around the world.

Camels—Sahara, Great Arabian, Syrian, and Gobi Deserts

Contrary to what you might have heard, camels do not store water in their humps. While they can drink more than 30 gallons (114 liters) of water in ten minutes and can hold as much as 65 gallons (247 liters), they store that water throughout their bodies.

Otherwise they'd be top-heavy and risk falling over. What's actually in the hump is fat.

Camels are mostly domesticated, like cows, especially the one-hump camel, the dromedary. However, there are small herds of wild Bactrian (two-hump) camels in the Gobi Desert.

SPEED DEMONS OF THE DESERT

Racing camels have a top speed of 40 miles per hour (64 kilometers per hour) for short distances. They can run at 25 mph (40 kph) for an hour, or a steady 12 mph (19 kph) for eighteen hours.

Lemmings—Arctic Desert

Most of us know at least one urban legend, but did you know there are also nature legends? Among these is the story of lemmings committing mass suicide, flinging themselves over cliffs when the lemming population gets too large. As wonderfully weird as this tale is, however, it's not true. While these small rodents do go through cycles of growth and decline, and sometimes migrate in large numbers in search of food, they don't kill themselves to make room for their descendants. Falling off cliffs occurs purely by accident.

Lemmings have to migrate because they are herbivores (they eat plants), and since the Arctic desert has so little available water to nourish plants, there actually aren't very many plants there.

In the winter, this Arctic lemming lives in burrows beneath the snow-covered Arctic desert. Though white in the winter (for camouflage), the rest of the year lemmings are gray or brown. Some of their most odd features—furry soles and ears that are concealed in their fur—help them deal with the harsh cold of Arctic winters. During the winter, they eat what leaves, twigs, and bark they can find.

Like their close relative, the vole, lemmings aren't very smart, and when migrating, they're unable to change direction if they encounter a cliff. What then happens is that there are so many lemmings behind them, that the front-runners get pushed over the edge. So while they do fall from cliffs to their deaths, it's certainly not because they choose to do so. They've also been known to drown while trying to cross the sea, which occurs because from their low height, the sea looks the same as a river, which they can cross.

Saguaros—Sonoran Desert

The saguaro (pronounced suh-WAR-uh) cactus is the largest cactus in the United States. Saguaros can grow to be as high as 50 feet (15.25 meters) tall, but it takes a very long time because they grow only a few inches (a dozen centimeters) a year. Saguaros don't develop "arms" until they're at least thirty years old, and sometimes they live as long as 200 years. Though rare, if you visit the Saguaro National Monument East or Saguaro National Monument West (both are close to the city of Tucson, Arizona), you'll see a lot of them.

Saguaros are the apartment complexes of the desert. When looking for bugs to eat, Gila woodpeckers bore holes into the sides of the cactus, then other birds move into the holes. There can be dozens of holes in a single saguaro, each containing a nest.

Tarantulas—Sonoran, Chihuahuan, and Mojave Deserts

Big furry spiders—it doesn't get much weirder than that. There are different

SUNSCREEN NEEDED

Just like humans, saguaros can get sunburned. That's why saguaros transplanted to Palm Springs, California, almost always die. The Mojave Desert is a lot hotter and drier than the Sonoran Desert, where the saguaro originates.

varieties of tarantulas, but they're all furry and big, with a leg span as large as 6 to 7 inches (15 to 17 centimeters). They live mostly in the deserts of the American Southwest but are found as far east in the United States as the Mississippi River.

Despite their appearance, they're actually quite shy. Just be wary—they attack their prey by jumping or pouncing on it. Though they may appear slow as they crawl across the ground, get too close and you might have one leap straight up at you. Another weird thing about them is they bite their food twice. The first bite is a "dry bite" without any venom. It's the second bite that contains the poison. Most tarantula bites are equivalent to a wasp or bee sting, but there are deadly varieties in Africa (baboon spiders) and southern Asia (ornamental tarantulas).

EEK! A TARANTULA!

If you find a tarantula crawling on you, be gentle. They're amazingly fragile. First find something to brush it off with— something soft like a sweatshirt or magazine, not a stick. (Don't use your hand. Their fur consists of barbed hairs that can stick in your skin and cause a rash.) If that doesn't work, stand up and gently jump up and down. It'll fall off and crawl away.

The most common type of tarantula in North America is the *Eurypelma californicum*. These tarantulas are found in California, Arizona (like the one pictured here), and Texas. Scientists know of one tarantula in this species that lived for thirty years! Some tarantulas can actually be trained as pets, but watch out for bites.

If you don't want to get bitten, don't tease or torment a tarantula, and definitely don't pick it up. A tarantula's usual diet consists of lizards, bugs, and even mice, so keep your fingers out of its reach as they might be mistaken for dinner. If a tarantula does bite you, clean the wound and bandage it. If the area of the bite swells or hurts for hours, you should see a doctor.

THE BIZARRE

Bizarre, like weird, includes "fantastic" within its definition, but it's more extreme, more sensational. Even a bit more strange and alien. See if you agree that the following desert plants truly are bizarre.

The Mojave Desert region of southeastern California and parts of Nevada, Arizona, and Utah is home to the famous Joshua tree (or the *Yucca brevifolia* in Latin—as they are referred to by scientists and botonists). Because these spiky-leafed evergreens do not grow anywhere else in the world, they have become a symbol of the Mojave Desert.

Joshua Trees— Mojave Desert

The Sonoran Desert is known for the saguaro cactus, the Chihuahuan Desert for the agave lechugilla (called the shindigger), and the Great Basin for sagebrush, but the most bizarre plant is the Joshua tree, the identifying plant of the Mojave Desert. The Joshua tree looks like an armored cactus, but it is in fact an oversized yucca. In 1844, explorer John C. Fremont called it "the most repulsive tree in the vegetable kingdom." It was the Mormons who named the tree, based on a Bible story of Joshua beckoning people to the promised land. The Mormons said that the uplifted branches were like the arms of Joshua.

Teddy Bear Chollas—Sonoran Desert

Another truly bizarre plant is the teddy bear cholla (pronounced CHOY-uh; it's Spanish). One of several varieties of cholla, it grows up to 5 feet (1.5 meters) tall, and the spines are so thickly packed that it looks furry, hence the name. It's not at all cute, however. The spines are so loosely attached that if you brush against the cholla, the spines seem to jump at you. You never get just one spine either; an entire clump of them will end up firmly attached to your shirt or jeans, or if you're very unlucky, to your skin. As if that's not sufficiently bizarre, the spines are barbed and so sharp that they'll pierce a bug trying to land on the cactus.

Removing cholla or any cactus needles from your skin is difficult, as nearly all the spines have barbs—like tiny fishhooks—that cling to you. Never use your bare hand to remove a chunk of cactus, especially cholla, as it simply spreads the pain and damage. Use pliers or tweezers to gently pull out the pieces and dispose of them, or even better, have someone else do it for you. For those tiny pieces you can't see, people who live in the Sonoran Desert for any length of time learn to use olive oil. They even use it on their

Though the teddy bear cholla (pictured above in New Mexico's Mojave Desert) was said to look like the fuzzy arms and legs of a stuffed teddy bear, it is not really something you would want to touch, much less hug. It can grow to a height of 5 to 9 feet (1.5 to 2.7 meters) and produces yellow egg-shaped fruit.

horses' legs! The oil softens the skin, and the spines and barbs loosen and fall out.

Welwitschia— Namib Desert

In the Namib Desert of Africa grows a bizarre-looking dwarf tree called welwitschia. It has a huge tap root over 5 feet (1.5 meters) wide with only two leathery green leaves that continue to grow all the plant's life. The slow-growing welwitschia lives for as long as 1,000 to 2,000 years.

The Namib is also called the Skeleton Coast due to the treacherous offshore reefs that rip out the hulls of ships, causing them to sink. While the desert itself is almost lifeless, the neighboring Atlantic Ocean is home to sea lions and otters, as well as great white sharks.

The Namib Desert—known as the world's oldest desert—is a remote desert coastline stretching 1,243 miles (2,000 km) from South Africa to Angola. It is here that the rare and amazing welwitschia dwarf tree grows. These plants were first discovered in the Angola desert by an Austrian botanist named Friederich Welwitsch in 1860. Once these plants are about twenty years old, they produce flowers that look like cones.

THE DEADLY

Deadly doesn't always mean instantly fatal. Sometimes it's merely the potential to cause death. In certain circumstances, each of the animals discussed below can kill you. If you encounter them, be careful.

Gila Monsters—Sonoran and Mojave Deserts

The Gila monster (pronounced HEE-luh; it's Spanish) is one of only two poisonous lizards in the world. (The other is the Mexican beaded lizard.) It's named for the Gila River Basin of the U.S. Southwest. While Gila monsters appear to be slow and sluggish, like an alligator or crocodile, they can make short dashes to attack prey. This means stay away from it if you spot one. Gila monsters move a lot faster than you probably

This reticulated Gila monster *(Heloderma suspectum)* lives in southern Arizona. Reticulated refers to the pattern of its skin. Gila monsters, which grow to be about twenty inches (fifty centimeters), feed on small mammals, birds, and eggs.

think they can. When they attack, they bite down on their prey and inject a nerve toxin (poison) through grooves in their teeth while gnawing on their victims. Gila monsters are deadly to animals but usually not to people.

Polar Bears—Greenland, Canada, United States, and Siberia

Polar bears are deadly not because they're poisonous, but because they're some of the best hunters on Earth. The largest bears on the planet, they grow up to 9 feet (2.7 meters) long and can weigh as much as 1,700 pounds (770 kilograms).

In summer they'll eat berries, leaves, and bird eggs, but their primary diet is meat. They hunt their own food and scavenge from the prey of others. They can run fast enough to chase and catch caribou, as well as smaller animals such as hares. They also swim well, using their front legs to paddle, catching fish, seals, and sea birds. According to Michael Allaby in *Biomes of the World, Volume 1: The Polar Regions*, "They have even been known to attack walruses and beluga whales."

Dangerous as polar bears are, they are now protected by international conservation programs because human hunters have killed so many of them. One of these protections is an agreement between the United States and Russia, signed in

2000, that prohibits commercial hunting and the use of aircraft to hunt bears, among other restrictions.

Scorpions—Sonoran, Mojave, Sahara, Syrian, and Great Arabian Deserts

The most frightening creatures in appearance are scorpions. Related to the spider, they've been around for more than 300 million years. But while they're all venomous, only a few are deadly to humans. Their normal prey includes spiders, grasshoppers, centipedes, small snakes, and even other scorpions. A scorpion attacks using the stinger on the tip of its tail, which contains venom that paralyzes its prey.

Most scorpion stings hurt but aren't deadly. One exception, the small bark scorpion, a common resident of the U.S. Southwest and Mexico, can be recognized by its pale strawlike color, its size (1.5 inches [4 centimeters] long when fully grown), and slender pincers. It's called the bark scorpion because its favorite home is the underside of wood, such as stacked logs, fallen tree branches, and yard debris.

Scorpions aren't always tiny either. The giant desert hairy scorpion can be up to 5 inches (13 centimeters) long, with the largest being the "long-tailed" South African scorpion, which can exceed 8 inches (20 centimeters). The

The giant hairy desert scorpion *(Hadrurus arizonensis)* pictured here is one of approximately 1,300 species of scorpions worldwide. While most scorpions actually have between three and eight pairs of eyes, some scorpions who live in caves are eyeless! Though they are most often associated with the desert, some scorpions have been found living under snow-covered rocks in the mountains.

deadliest varieties live in North Africa, the Middle East, South America, India, and Mexico.

If you get stung, pay attention to how you feel. If you have breathing problems or numbness, seek medical help immediately. There are antivenins available.

CHAPTER TWO

WHERE NO ONE COULD SURVIVE— PEOPLE OF THE DESERT

What do you think of when you hear the phrase "people of the desert"? The black-robed Bedouins of the Arabian Desert? The Aborigines of the Australian outback? They're only two of the many groups of indigenous people who've found ways to survive in some of the most extreme environments on the planet.

INDIGENOUS PEOPLES

Despite the temperature extremes and survival difficulties, there have always been those who live in deserts. Where there is any water at all, people will find a way to survive.

The Aborigines of Australia

The Aborigines survive in one of the harshest deserts: the outback of Australia. Because there are no native animals suitable for herding (thus providing a constant food supply), Aborigines have had to learn how to hunt and what to eat. They use throwing spears and boomerangs, which have a range of up to 295 feet (90 meters), to target animals such as kangaroos, and they have discovered that they can eat the nutritious grubs found in tree roots. They rely on the moisture obtained from plants when no other water is available.

Aborigines have lived in Australia for at least 50,000 years, millennia before the first Europeans arrived. Paintings, stories, and songs passed from generation to generation record much of their knowledge, including routes across the

This close-up view of an Aboriginal petroglygh—a prehistoric rock carving or engraving—was photographed in the outback of Western Australia. Dating back approximately 2,000 years, this petroglyph gives anthropologists valuable insight into the culture of Aborigines. In this region of Australia, it is estimated that about 10,000 of such rock carvings exist.

This Bedouin falconer holds a Saker falcon in Qatar, a small country that borders Saudi Arabia. Falconry has thrived in the Middle East since before the ninth century, and the prey that falcons catch add variety to the Bedouin diet.

interior of Australia, the locations of sacred caves, and sources of food and water.

The Bedouin of Arabia

"Bedouin" means "desert dweller" in Arabic, though it applies only to those nomads who live in Arabia, the Negev, and the Sinai. (See the section on the Tuaregs for the nomads of the Sahara.) Because water and grass for their herds of sheep, goats, and camels are so scarce, they move from oasis to oasis, careful never to exhaust an area beyond nature's ability to replenish it by the time they return.

They raise ordinary camels and racing camels, plus Arabian horses (though many have been exported because of the politics in the region, to the point where some Arabian princes come to the United States to obtain horses of the old blood). Bedouins also train peregrine falcons to hunt and retrieve hares and birds.

The Bedouin live in tents, and although they defend their territory, sometimes violently because of the scarcity of resources, they also have a strong custom of hospitality to guests. Though many have now settled in villages, others continue the traditional, nomadic life.

The Inuit of the Arctic

The Inuit, sometimes referred to as Eskimos, live in the Arctic regions of Greenland, northern Canada, and eastern Siberia. Parts of those regions are polar desert, hence the Inuit survive by hunting and by fishing. "Eskimo" means "raw fish eaters" and is a term that is generally no longer used.

The Mongolians of Central Asia

The Mongolians have traditionally been nomads, herding sheep, goats, cattle, and two-humped (Bactrian) camels for a living. They travel with their herds across the semiarid grasslands and

A Mongolian nomad walks between yurts in the Gobi Desert in Mongolia. Though this photo was taken in 1961, the Mongolian culture and way of life remains largely the same today.

fringes of the Gobi Desert. Today, many Mongolians live in permanent houses in the winter but continue a nomadic life in the summer. In the summer, they live in traditional, circular tents called *gers* or *yurts*, which are well-insulated (unlike the modern back-packing tent), and have changed little since the Middle Ages.

Native Americans

Across the Southwest and Great Basin, Native American tribes adapted to their environment, carving out their own

This Kalahari Bushman plays an unusual instrument, which consists partly of ostrich eggs hollowed out and filled with water. The Bushmen are adept at using the materials around them to create whatever tools and objects they need.

ecological niches. Among them are the Dîné (Navajo), Apache, Ute, Hopi, and Zuni. It was the Dîné who provided the U.S. government with a code language the Japanese army could not decipher during World War II.

Each group adapted to their own area, whether that meant using Arizona's Salt and Gila Rivers to grow crops, herding sheep, or learning to use every single bit of accessible plant life. As archaeologist Kent V. Flannery was quoted in *American Indian Food and Lore*, "They appear as a practiced and ingenious team of lay botanists who know how to wring the most out of a superficially bleak environment."

The San of the Kalahari

The San (also called Bushmen) are nomadic hunter-gatherers. They settle in an area where there is enough local game to hunt and vegetation to eat. Once supplies become scarce, they move on. The San use grass, leaves, and branches to make their homes. On a trek, they may bury water-filled ostrich eggs to drink on the return journey.

When they hunt, they coat their arrow points with a poison made of ground-up scarab beetles and plants. This is what enables them to hunt such food as giraffes—some of the only prey available in winter when the Kalahari is not just dry but cold (below freezing), and plants and animals become scarce.

The Tuaregs of the Sahara

The Tuaregs are the nomadic people of the southern Sahara Desert. They are known as "the blue people" because they wear distinctive dark blue clothing and the indigo dye rubs off onto their skin. Traditionally, the Tuaregs raise cattle and dromedaries, and cross the Sahara with caravans carrying gold, ivory, salt, ebony, and spices, going from water hole to water hole. Today, some are still nomads, while others are settled into cities and villages.

They not only have their own language, Tamashek, a Berber dialect, but they have their own writing system called Tifinar. In addition, unlike the usual image of people of North Africa and the Middle East (where the women are veiled), it's the Tuareg men who go veiled. They cover their faces in the presence of women, strangers, and in-laws.

IMMIGRANTS

A lot of people seek out deserts and choose to live there permanently, regardless of the challenges of living is such an environment.

This Xeriscape garden consists of succulents and other plants that have a high tolerance for heat and dryness. "Xeriscape" is taken from the Greek word "xeros," meaning "dry."

Welcome to the Desert Southwest

Among the places in the United States with the fastest-growing populations are California, Arizona, and Nevada. The climate attracts a lot of people who are tired of ice, blizzards, and other cold-weather challenges found in large parts of the United States and Canada. Many of these people try to retain the look of their previous homes, resulting in high water usage as they insist on green lawns and large gardens. Others adapt, at least in part, by creating Xeriscape gardens, which use drought-tolerant plants, gravel, and decorative rocks.

Swimming pools and golf courses are other ways the desert is being changed by new arrivals. However, not all golf courses are "water hogs." Many of them use "gray water," which is reclaimed water from the sewage system that is clean enough to use on plants but not clean enough to drink. This saves water and money for the community.

The Astronomers of the World

While there are astronomical observatories all over the world, some of the most utilized are in deserts because of the lack of humidity in the air and the high percentage of nights without clouds to obscure the skies, which makes the stars easier to see. Among the better known are Kitt Peak National Observatory in the Sonoran Desert west of Tucson, Arizona, and the Paranal Observatory two hours north of Antofagasta in the Atacama Desert of Chile. The Paranal Observatory has the VLT (very large telescope), consisting of four 323-inch (8.2-meter) telescopes, plus three smaller ones in combination, mimicking one massive 7,874-inch (200-meter) telescope.

DESERTS BY REGION
North America

DESERT	AREA	COMMENTS
Canadian Arctic	The far northeast of Canada including the Brodeur Peninsula	Also referred to as the Arctic Cordillera.
Chihuahuan Desert	Mexico, Texas, New Mexico	Includes Big Bend National Park.
Great Basin Desert	Utah, Nevada, Idaho, Oregon, Colorado, Arizona, Washington, Canada	Includes the Painted Desert in the Four Corners area where Utah, Arizona, New Mexico, and Colorado meet, and the Great Salt Lake.
Mojave Desert	California, Arizona, Nevada	The hottest temperature ever recorded in the United States occurred in Death Valley on July 10, 1913, when it hit 134° F (56.7° C) at Greenland Ranch.
Sonoran Desert	Mexico, Arizona, California	When Phoenix, Arizona, hit 122° F (50° C) on June 26, 1990, Skyharbor Airport was closed because of the heat. Planes already on their way to Phoenix had to land at Tucson International Airport, where it was a cooler 117° F (47.2° C).

A *bajada* (a sloping, gravelly area) in the Organ Pipe Cactus National Monument in Arizona, part of the Sonoran Desert

South America

DESERT	AREA	COMMENTS
Monte Desert	Northwestern Argentina	Includes the Biosphere Reserve of Nacuñan.
Patagonian Desert	Southern Argentina	More than a hundred million years ago, this was a steamy jungle filled with dinosaurs.
Atacama Desert	Northern coast of Chile	One of the driest places on Earth, with an average annual precipitation of 0.03 inches (0.76 mm), recorded over the past 59 years at Arica.
Peruvian Desert	Peru	Ancient drawings are etched into the desert's surface, forming enormous animals and geometric patterns.

An eroded (worn away by water, wind, and ice) landscape shows the layers of rock beneath the hills of the desert in Patagonia, Argentina.

Middle East

DESERT	AREA	COMMENTS
Great Arabian Desert	Saudi Arabia, United Arab Emirates, Oman, Yemen, Qatar	The area is mostly known for vast fields of oil and natural gas.
Negev	Southern Israel	Includes Ein Ovdat National Park.
Syrian Desert	Syria, Iraq, Saudi Arabia, Jordan	Covers more than half of the country of Syria.
Wadi Rum	Jordan	Here the police patrol with camels, not jeeps or horses.

Africa

DESERT	AREA	COMMENTS
Egyptian Desert	Egypt	Fed by unusually high levels of rainfall and water overflowing from the Aswan High Dam on the Nile River, the first of four new lakes appeared in 1998.
Libyan Desert	Libya, Egypt, Sudan	Highest recorded temperature in the entire world was noted here: 136° F (57.8° C) on September 13, 1922, in the town of El Azizia.
Nubian Desert	Northeastern Sudan	Bordered by the Nile River on the west and the Red Sea on the east.
Sahara Desert	Northern Africa	The world's largest desert, covering approximately 3,500,000 square miles (9,000,000 square km).
Somali Chalbi	Somalia, Ethiopia, Kenya	Badly affected by years of drought, this desert gets drier every year.
Kalahari Desert	Botswana, South Africa, Namibia, Angola, Zimbabwe, Zambia	Includes three of Africa's most remote game reserves: the Central Kalahari Game Reserve, Khutse Game Reserve, and Gemsbok National Park.
Karoo Desert	South Africa	Includes the Great Karoo and Little Karoo.
Namib Desert	Namibia—Southwest coastal Africa	Borders the Atlantic Ocean, which provides cold and dampness to create fog, the only accessible moisture.

A fossilized riverbed stretching across the African Kalahari

Asia

DESERT	AREA	COMMENTS
Gobi Desert	Mongolia and northern China	The remote mountain ranges are among the richest dinosaur fossil sites in the world.
Iranian Desert	Iran, Afghanistan, Pakistan	Includes the world's largest salt flat.
Siberia	Eastern Russia tundra above Arctic Circle	The winter storms that cross the Pacific Ocean to dump rain and snow on the western United States and Canada begin as continental polar air masses over the Siberian Desert.
Takla Makan Desert	Western China	The common translation into English is "Place from which there is no return." The literal meaning is "buried city."
Thar Desert	Western India and Pakistan	In May 1974, India exploded its first nuclear device at Pokhran in the Thar Desert.
Turkestan Desert	East of Caspian Sea	Sometimes split into the Kara Kum between the Caspian Sea and the Aral Sea, and the Kyzul Kum east of the Aral Sea.

Antarctica

DESERT	AREA	COMMENTS
Antarctic	Antarctica	Amundsen-Scott South Pole Station has an average rainfall of 0.8 inches (20.3 mm) a year, making it the third driest place on the planet. The thermometer has dipped as low as minus 129° F (-89.4° C)

Australia

DESERT	AREA	COMMENTS
Gibson Desert	Western Australia, below Tropic of Capricorn	One early explorer called it a "great undulating desert of gravel."
Great Sandy Desert	Western Australia, above Tropic of Capricorn	Includes Wolf Creek Meteor Crater Reserve.
Great Victoria Desert	Western Australia, South Australia	In 1875, British explorer Ernest Giles, the first European to cross the desert, named it after the British queen at the time, Queen Victoria.
Simpson Desert	Queensland, Northern Territory, South Australia	Includes Queensland's Simpson Desert National Park, South Australia's Simpson Desert Conservation Park, and Simpson Desert Regional Reserve.
Tanami Desert	Northern Territory, Western Australia	Includes the Old Granite Gold Mine, featuring the original 1930s buildings and workings.

CHAPTER THREE

LOST IN THE DESERT— COULD YOU SURVIVE?

According to adventurer, author, and survival teacher Charles A. Lehman in his *Desert Survival Handbook*, "Survival is really nothing more than managing your own mind and body in an unusual or hostile environment—and you can find yourself in that position, no matter who you are or what you do." In *The Extreme Survival Guide*, Australian Rory Storm explains it in a similar way: "Surviving comes in many guises. It's not simply about you against the elements. It's to do with how you react in an unfamiliar and potentially dangerous situation, what inner strengths you draw on in the face of adversity, the skills you have and how you use them, not to mention courage and determination."

In other words, your mental state matters even more than your knowledge of survival techniques. Panic, and you give up. If you keep your wits about you and stop to think before, during, and after the realization that you're lost or stranded, you have a much better chance of seeing family and friends again.

Hiking in deserts like this one, the Atacama Desert in Chile, requires preparation and caution. Every year, some hikers end up lost, injured, or worse because they took unnecessary risks.

FIRST THINGS FIRST

No matter how you got into the desert, if you're unable to get out as planned, the first thing to do is take an inventory of what you have with you. If you have a cell phone, then immediately check to see if it works where you are. If you have a signal, stay put and use the phone to call for help. (Unfortunately, even if the phone's battery is charged, sometimes hills, trees, or lack of transmitters can prevent their use.) If the phone doesn't work or you don't have one, you'll have to find some other way to acquire assistance.

As it is incredibly easy to get lost, almost every search and rescue volunteer will tell you to stay where you are. This is especially true if you're with a vehicle (car, truck, bike). It's larger than you are and therefore much easier to spot by searchers. Next, find some way to signal for help, whether it's flashing sunlight using a mirror (or some other reflective surface), using a flashlight at night, or blowing a whistle (better to use a police whistle than puckering up).

If you made the mistake of not telling anyone where you were going—meaning that no one will know where to look for you if you don't make it back—signaling becomes even more important. Please note that a signal fire is not recommended. While there are times a fire is useful, especially if the desert you're lost in is the Arctic, it's all too easy for a fire to cause an even bigger problem.

The Rodeo-Chediski Fire

An excellent example of not being prepared and the bad things that can happen as a result occurred in the summer of 2002 in Arizona. According to an Associated Press interview, Valinda Elliott and her employer, Ransford Olmstead, became lost while driving between Phoenix and Young,

Arizona. Young is a very small town, difficult to locate, and since it was a last-minute decision, they hadn't done their homework to find out how to get there. Then they ran out of gas.

There was no cell phone signal so they couldn't call for help. They spent the first night sleeping in the vehicle. The following morning, wearing a tank top, shorts, and flip-flop sandals, Elliott left Olmstead and the vehicle to find a

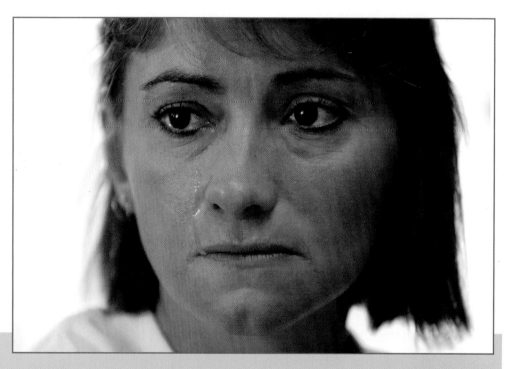

Valinda Elliott told the Associated Press that she couldn't believe the signal fire she started became part of an inferno that scorched nearly 469,000 acres (almost 2,000 square km) in Arizona. Elliott received intense criticism for her mistake.

place where her cell phone worked. Apparently, after walking most of the day, she realized she had lost sight of the road. She tried to signal for help from passing helicopters, but no one saw her. She said she drank water from muddy pools and didn't have any food.

Members of the "Sierra Hotshots" firefighting crew from California help hold the fire line near Cibecue, Arizona, during the Rodeo-Chediski fire. Fire crews from all over the United States flew in to help fight the enormous blaze.

The following day, after hearing a helicopter and trying to get its attention, she used a cigarette lighter to set fire to a small bush. The fire was spotted and she was rescued, a full day after her boss was found. Unfortunately, before fire crews could arrive to put out the fire she'd started, that one burning bush became the Chediski fire. Within days it merged with the nearby Rodeo fire to become the nearly half-million acre (2,000 square kilometers) Rodeo-Chediski fire, the largest wildfire in Arizona history—it destroyed at least 467 homes. This was all because of a series of mistakes that started with getting lost, and was made even worse by leaving the vehicle, not carrying water, and walking off the road without any hiking gear and no signaling device.

THINGS TO HAVE

There are some basic items to have with you whether you're in a car, on a dirt bike, or on foot. These include a cell phone (with the battery charged), a gallon of water per day per person, a jacket, and a hat. Ideally, you'll also have a flashlight, a small mirror and/or whistle (for signaling), a couple of plastic garbage bags for emergency shelter, and in case your cell phone won't work, quarters for a pay phone.

You should also tell someone where you're going, so if you don't make it back on time, search and rescue teams will have somewhere to start looking.

WHAT ABOUT EMERGENCIES?

If your car has broken down, stay with it and don't go wandering. However, if you were hiking or mountain biking and your best friend just broke a leg, fell down a cliff, or got bitten by a snake, for example, you'll need to get help as fast as you can. This is another reason to keep a cell phone with you. It's a much better idea to keep your friend company than leave him or her alone while you go off looking for help.

But if it's an absolute worst-case scenario, and you believe you have to find help, here are some suggestions:

1. Mark your trail so you can find your friend again. It doesn't help to find assistance then be unable to figure out where you were and where your friend is.

2. Keep track of directions. Remember, the sun and moon both rise in the East and set in the West. If it's night and you're in the Northern Hemisphere, use the Big Dipper to find Polaris (the North Star) to figure out directions. The two end stars on the bowl of the dipper point at the North Star, which is the last star in the handle of the slightly less visible Little Dipper. In the Southern Hemisphere, the Southern Cross is used, but it's not always visible in the night sky, so it's better to watch the sun and moon.

3. Leave water with your friend, but take water with you, too. If you become dehydrated, you can't help anyone.

4. It's better to follow marked trails than to go cross-country. Anything that looks like a shortcut probably isn't. The risk of twisting an ankle, falling, getting bitten by a snake, or running into a cactus is much higher off trails than on them.

OTHER SUGGESTIONS

- If you don't have a hat, make one from the end of your shirt, a rag, or something else. Always have extra water. A single water bottle is good only for an hour of hiking. If you're going any farther than that, you need more.

- If it's hot, find shade between 10 AM and 4 PM. You may have to move around to stay in shadows, but remaining out in the sun at the hottest part of the day is just plain dumb. However, *never* sit down without paying attention to what's around you. Snakes, scorpions, cactus spines, and other things can be not just uncomfortable but potentially deadly.

Finding Water

There is water out in the desert, but building a solar still or knowing where to dig can be complicated. Check out the survival books listed in the For Further Reading section at the back of this book for detailed instructions.

Please, do not look for a barrel cactus thinking to cut the top off to get at the water inside. While there is liquid inside the cactus, it contains oxalic acid, which causes nausea and will make you throw up. You'll be even more thirsty than before.

Finding Food

Unless you know what you're doing and can identify plants accurately, you're as likely to make yourself sick as obtain nourishment. The exception is if you're with an adult who's an expert on desert survival, but not many are. Humans can go for more than a week with no food, so focus on signaling for help and being rescued.

A barrel cactus with yellow blooms in the Sonoran Desert of Arizona. Many desert animals will eat the fruit of barrel cacti. Pack rats also use the cactus for shelter.

Was That a Deadly Scorpion?

There are obvious differences between the feel of an ordinary scorpion sting and that of a deadly scorpion. The non-lethal variety will cause pain, swelling, and discoloration at the site of the sting, sometimes extending toward the center of the body. If it's a lethal sting, there is likely to be immediate pain at the site, but the pain recedes and there's no swelling or bruising. You won't be able to see where it occurred; the bite itself will be invisible. However, the site will become

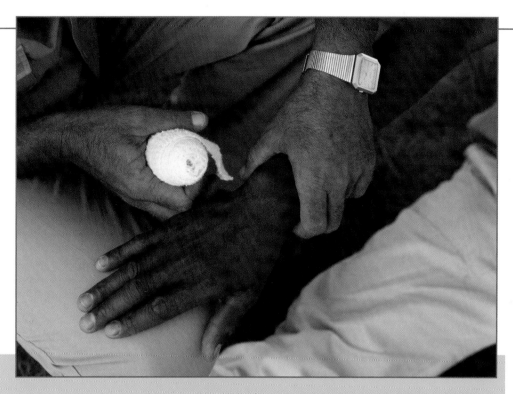

Between 7,000 and 8,000 people a year receive venomous bites in the United States, and about 5 of those people die. Some experts say that because people who are bitten can't always positively identify a snake, they should seek prompt care for any bite, though they may not think the snake is poisonous. Even a bite from a so-called harmless snake can cause an infection or allergic reaction in some individuals.

hypersensitive to any pressure or movement and then it will tingle, prickle, or just plain hurt a lot.

Snake Bite

There are antivenins available, so keep yourself or the person stung calm and get medical help as quickly as possible.

Pack It Out

The desert is dangerous, even deadly, but you can do harm to it as well. Everything you take into the desert should come back out with you. Because the desert is so dry, things don't decompose like in forests; they'll be there for a century or more. Disgusting as it sounds, you should also pack out any used toilet paper and bodily waste. Plastic bags are your best friend in this situation.

   The single most important survival tool is your brain. If you think through what you'd do in a situation, you're more likely to do the smart thing if or when it actually happens. Give getting stranded or lost in the desert (or any extreme environment) some thought. It may not only save your life someday but the lives of people you care about.

GLOSSARY

antivenin An antitoxin for snake venom or other animal poisons.

Arctic The region around the North Pole, north of the Arctic Circle.

biome A natural community of living things that covers a large area, with the emphasis on the plant life, hence names such as grassland or forest.

ecosystem The complex interrelated system of plants and animals that occupy a particular physical area, whether urban or remote desert.

habitat The environment a particular organism (plant or animal) usually occupies, or an area distinguished by the group of plants and animals that live there.

herbivores Animals that eat only plants, like rabbits and antelopes.

nomads People who have a wandering lifestyle, moving from place to place rather than settling in one spot.

oasis A place in the desert where there is water, often from an underground spring. Usually an oasis is permanent, but it can dry up. In the Arctic, however, it means an ice-free area.

tap root A central root growing vertically downward from which small rootlets extend into the soil.

tundra A cold, treeless plain near the top of the world.

wadi A steep-sided valley formed by flash flooding in dry regions during a heavy rainstorm. Also used for any Saharan or Arabian Desert streambed that is usually dry except during the rainy season. (They're called washes in the American Southwest.)

Xeriscape Landscaping or gardens designed for dry conditions, whether drought or desert.

yurts Tents for the nomads of the Gobi Desert.

FOR MORE INFORMATION

Bryce Canyon National Park
P.O. Box 170001
Bryce Canyon, UT 84717
(435) 834-5322
Web site: http://www.nps.gov/brca/home.htm

Cabeza Prieta National Wildlife Refuge
1611 North Second Avenue
Ajo, AZ 85321
(520) 387-6483
Web site: http://southwest.fws.gov/refuges/arizona/
   cabeza.html

Chihuahuan Desert
P.O. Box 129
Big Bend National Park, TX 79834
(915) 477-2251
Web site: http://www.nps.gov/bibe/home.htm

Death Valley National Park
P.O. Box 579
Death Valley, CA 92328
(760) 786-3200
Web site: http://www.nps.gov/deva

Dinosaur National Monument
4545 East Highway 40
Dinosaur, CO 81610-7924

Headquarters: (970) 374-3000
Visitor Information: (970) 781-7700
Web site: http://www.nps.gov/dino

Grand Canyon National Park
P.O. Box 129
Grand Canyon, AZ 86023
(928) 638-7888
Web site: http://www.nps.gov/grca/grandcanyon

Great Basin Desert
Arches National Park
P.O. Box 907
Moab, UT 84532
Headquarters: (435) 719-2100
Visitor Information: (435) 719-2299
Web site: http://www.nps.gov/arch

Great Basin National Park
100 Great Basin National Park
Baker, NV 89311
(702) 234-7331
Web site: http://www.nps.gov/grba/home.htm

Joshua Tree National Park
74485 National Park Drive
Twenty-nine Palms, CA 92277-3597
(760) 367-5500
Web site: http://www.nps.gov/jotr

Mojave Desert State Parks
43779 15th Street West
Lancaster, CA 93534
(661) 942-0662
Web site: http://www.calparksmojave.com

Mojave National Preserve
222 East Main Street, Suite 202
Barstow, CA 92311
(760) 255-8800
Web site: http://www.nps.gov/moja

Parks Canada National Office
25 Eddy Street
Hull, PQ K1A 0M5
Canada
(888) 900-0001
Web site: http://www.pch.gc.ca/pc-ch/ac-os/pc_e.cfm

Saguaro National Park
3693 South Old Spanish Trail
Tucson, AZ 85730
(520) 733-5153 (East)
(520) 733-5158 (West)
Web site: http://www.nps.gov/sagu

Sonoran Desert
Arizona-Sonora Desert Museum
2021 North Kinney Road

Tucson, AZ 85743
(520) 883-1380
Web site: http://www.desertmuseum.org

White Sands National Monument
P.O. Box 1086
Holloman Air Force Base (AFB), NM 88330
(505) 479-6124
Web site: http://www.nps.gov/whsa

WWF (World Wildlife Federation) Canada
245 Eglinton Avenue East, Suite 410
Toronto, ON M4P 3J1
Canada
(800) 26-PANDA (267-2632)
Web site: http://www.wwfcanada.org

WEB SITES

Due to the changing nature of Internet links, the Rosen Publishing Group, Inc., has developed an online list of Web sites related to the subject of this book. This site is updated regularly. Please use this link to access the list:

http://www.rosenlinks.com/lee/dese

FOR FURTHER READING

Allaby, Michael. *Deserts*. Danbury, CT: Grolier Educational, 1999.

Allaby, Michael. *The Polar Regions*. Danbury, CT: Grolier Educational, 1999.

Arnold, Caroline, and Arthur Arnold, photographer. *Watching Desert Wildlife*. Minneapolis, MN: Carolrhoda Books, Inc., 1994.

Grubbs, Bruce. *Desert Hiking Tips—Expert Advice on Desert Hiking and Driving*. Helena, MT: Falcon Publishing, 1998.

Gunzi, Christiane. *The Best Book of Polar Animals*. New York: Kingfisher Publications, 2002.

Hunt, Joni Phelps. *The Desert*. San Luis Obispo, CA: Blake Publishing, 1991.

Lazaroff, David Wentworth. *Arizona-Sonora Desert Museum Book of Answers*. Tucson, AZ: Arizona-Sonora Desert Museum Press, 1998.

Lehman, Charles A. *Desert Survival Handbook*. Phoenix: Primer Publishers, 1998.

Le Rochais, Marie-Ange. Translated from the French by George L. Newman. *Desert Trek: An Eye-Opening Journey Through the World's Driest Places*. New York: Walker & Company, 1999.

Piven, Joshua, and David Borgenicht. *The Worst-Case Scenario Survival Handbook: Travel*. San Francisco: Chronicle Books, 2001.

Ruth, Maria Mudd. *The Deserts of the Southwest* (Ecosystems of North America). New York: Benchmark Books, 1999.

Steele, Christy. *Deserts*. Austin, TX: Steck-Vaughn Company, 2001.

Storm, Rory. *The Extreme Survival Guide!* Boston: Element Children's Books, 1999.

Wallace, Marianne D. *America's Deserts: Guide to Plants and Animals*. Golden, CO: Fulcrum Publishing, 1996.

BIBLIOGRAPHY

Adventure Center, North Vancouver Island. "The Grizzly Bear (Ursus Arctos Horribilis)." Retrieved October 21, 2002 (http://www.adventurecenter.ca/links/grizzleyinfo.html).

Alcock, John. *Sonoran Desert Spring.* Chicago: University of Chicago Press, 1985.

Allaby, Michael. *Deserts* (Biomes of the World). Danbury, CT: Grolier Educational, 1999.

Allaby, Michael. *The Polar Regions* (Biomes of the World). Danbury, CT: Grolier Educational, 1999.

Alloway, David. *Desert Survival Skills.* Austin, TX: University of Texas Press, 2000.

Arnold, Caroline, and Arthur Arnold, photographer. *Watching Desert Wildlife.* Minneapolis, MN, Carolrhoda Books, Inc., 1994.

Baker, Janet. "Frequently Asked Gardening Questions." *The Desert Leaf*, October 2002, p. 28.

Barrios, Joseph. *Arizona Daily Star.* "Prosecutor cites lack of evidence of criminal intent." July 19, 2002. Retrieved November 12, 2002 (http://www.azstarnet.com/wildfire/20719CHEDISKIFIRE.html).

Blackwood, Alisa. *Arizona Daily Star*, July 12, 2002. Retrieved November 12, 2002 (http://www.azstarnet.com/wildfire/20712RLostWoman2f2fdst2fgc.html).

Brice-Bennett, Carol. Memorial University of Newfoundland. "The Inuit." Retrieved October 21, 2002 (http://www.heritage.nf.ca/aboriginal/inuit.html).

Brook, Larry. *Daily Life in Ancient and Modern Timbuktu.* Minneapolis, MN: Runestone Press, 1999.

Canada Terrain Sciences Division. "Brodeur Peninsula." Retrieved June 10, 2002 (http://sts.gsc.nrcan.gc.ca/page1/landf/ne/baffin/brodeur/nice.htm).

Canada Yearbook 1999. "Ecozone." Retrieved June 10, 2002. (http://statcan.gc.ca/english/kits/cyb1999/ecozone/art1.htm).

Canadian Heritage, Parks Canada. "Eastern High Arctic Glacier Natural Region." Retrieved June 10, 2002 (http://www.parcscanada.gc.ca/natress/inf_pa1/ECO_DES/NAT_REG/nat_r39e.htm).

Canadian Heritage, Parks Canada. "Western High Arctic Natural Region." Retrieved June 10, 2002 (http://www.parcscanada.gc.ca/natress/inf_pa1/ECO_DES/NAT_REG/nat_r38e.htm).

Catch Water Newsletter. "Cholistan's Story." December 2000. Retrieved November 12, 2002. (http://www.rainwaterharvesting.org/catchwater/apr2001/research_paper.htm).

CIA, *The World Factbook*. "Elevation Extremes." Retrieved September 28, 2002 (http://www.cia.gov/cia/publications/factbook).

Desert USA. "Scorpions." Retrieved September 30, 2002 (http://www.desertusa.com/oct96/du_scorpion.html).

Fouquette, M. J. Arizona State University. "Life Sciences, Biology 428 Biogeography: Lecture Outlines, Part 1." Retrieved June 7, 2002 (http://lsvl.la.asu.edu/bio428/Outlines/1.10.deserts.html).

Fouquette, M. J. Arizona State University. "Major Deserts of the World —Northern Hemisphere." Retrieved June 7, 2002 (http://lsvl.la.asu.edu/bio428/Outlines/1.10.1NHdeserts.html).

Fouquette, M. J. Arizona State University. "Major Deserts of the World – Southern Hemisphere." Retrieved June 7, 2002 (http://lsvl.la.asu.edu/bio428/Outlines/1.10.2SHdeserts.html).

Fowler, Allan. *It Could Still Be a Desert*. New York: Children's Press, 1997.

Fowler, Allan. *Living in a Desert*. New York: Children's Press, 2000.

Ganci, Dave. *Desert Hiking*. Berkeley, CA: Wilderness Press, 1979. Second printing November 1988.

Geographia. "The Bedouin. Culture in Transition." Retrieved October 21, 2002 (http://www.geographia.com/egypt/sinai/bedouin.htm).

Geological Survey of Canada. "Terrain Sciences." Retrieved September 29, 2002 (http://sts.gsc.nrcan.gc.ca).

Grubbs, Bruce. *Desert Hiking Tips—Expert Advice on Desert Hiking and Driving*. Helena, MT: Falcon Publishing, 1998.

Gunzi, Christiane. *The Best Book of Polar Animals*. New York: Kingfisher Publications, 2002.

Hunt, Joni Phelps. *The Desert*. San Luis Obispo, CA: Blake Publishing, 1991.

Inuit Art Foundation. "Canadian Arctic Multimedia Information Kit." Retrieved June 10, 2002 (http://www.schoolnet/ca/aboriginal/camik/menu1-e.html).

Inuit Circumpolar Conference. "General Information." Retrieved October 21, 2002 (http://www.inuit.org).

Johnson, Rebecca L. Illustrated by Phyllis V. Saroff. *A Walk in the Tundra*. Minneapolis, MN: Carolrhoda Books, Inc., 2001.

Larson, Peggy and Lane Larson. *The Deserts of the Southwest*, 2nd edition (A Sierra Club Naturalist's Guide). San Francisco, CA: Sierra Club Books, 1990.

Lazaroff, David Wentworth. *Arizona-Sonora Desert Museum Book of Answers*. Tucson, AZ: Arizona-Sonora Desert Museum Press, 1998.

Lehman, Charles A. *Desert Survival Handbook*. Phoenix, AZ: Primer Publishers, 1998.

Lerner, Carol. *A Desert Year*. New York: Morrow Junior Books, 1991.

Le Rochais, Marie-Ange. Translated from the French by George L. Newman. *Desert Trek: An Eye-Opening Journey Through the World's Driest Places*. New York: Walker & Company, 1999.

Lonely Planet. "Lonely Planet Theme Guides—Deserts." Retrieved June 10, 2002 (http://www.lonelyplanet.com/theme/deserts/deserts_index).

McGourty, Christine. BBC News. "Big Eye on the Sky." July 6, 2002. Retrieved July 7, 2002 (http://news.bbc.co.uk/hi/english/sci/tech/newsid_2098000/2099630.stm).

McGourty, Christine. BBC News. "Perfect for Washing and Astronomy." July 7, 2002. Retrieved July 7, 2002 (http://news.bbc.co.uk/hi/english/sci/tech/newsid_2098000/2098910.stm).

Murray, John A. *Cactus Country: An Illustrated Guide*. Boulder, CO: Roberts Rinehart Publishers, 1996.

National Wildlife Federation. "Polar Bear." Retrieved October 21, 2002 (http://www.nwf.org/keepthewildalive/polarbear.cfm).

NCDC. "Global Measured Extremes of Temperature and Precipitation." Retrieved September 28, 2002 (http://lwf.ncdc.noaa.gov/oa/climate/globalextremes.html).

O'Bryan, Aileen. Bulletin 163 of the Bureau of American Ethnology of the Smithsonian Institution [1956]. "The Dîné: Origin Myths of the Navaho Indians." Retrieved October 21, 2002 (http://www.sacred-texts.com/nam/nav/omni).

Oldershaw, Cally. *Deserts and Wastelands* (Closer Look At). Brookfield, CT: Copper Beech Books, 1999.

Parks Canada. Retrieved November 13, 2002 (http://parkscanada.pch.gc.ca/parks/main_e.htm).

Ruth, Maria Mudd. *The Deserts of the Southwest* (Ecosystems of North America). New York: Benchmark Books, 1999.

Science@NASA. "Space Medicine." Retrieved September 30, 2002 (http://science.nasa.gov/headlines/y2002/30sept_spacemedicine.htm?list627137).

Simon Fraser University, Vancouver, British Columbia. "Earth Science Links." Retrieved June 10, 2002 (http://www.sfu.ca/earth-sciences/EarthInk.htm).

Tilton, Buck. Michael Hodgson's Adventure Network. "Scorpion Stings: Avoidance and First Aid Tips." Retrieved October 21, 2002 (http://www.adventurenetwork.com/Healthsafe/Scorpionsting.html).

Wallace, Marianne D. *America's Deserts: Guide to Plants and Animals*. Golden, CO: Fulcrum Publishing, 1996.

INDEX

San (Bushmen), 30–31
scorpions, 22–23, 46
  bites/stings of, 47–48
Siberia, 21, 28, 37
Skeleton Coast, 18
snake bites, 45, 46, 48
Sonoran Desert, 13, 16, 17, 20,
    22, 33, 34
Southwest (U.S.), 14, 20, 22,
    29, 32
survival techniques, 39–41,
    44–46, 49
  finding food, 47
  finding water, 46
  things to have, 44
Syrian Desert, 10, 22, 35

T

tarantulas, 13–15
  bites of, 14
teddy bear chollas, 17–18
temperature, 5–6, 7, 9, 25,
    34, 36
Tuaregs, 27, 31–32

U

United States, 7, 13, 14, 20, 21,
    22, 28, 29–30
  fastest-growing populations of, 32
Ute, 30

V

voles, 12

W

water, 6, 10, 11, 25, 27, 32, 33,
    44, 45
  finding, 46
welwitschia, 18

X

Xeriscape gardens, 32

Y

yucca, 16
yurts, 29

Z

Zuni, 30

About the Author

Katherine Lawrence has had more than thirty television scripts produced, most recently for *Stargate Infinity*. She was nominated for a Writers Guild of America Award in 1997 for her "Ice Bound" episode of the ABC series Hypernauts. Other credits include writing computer games, short stories, and a book on actor/martial artist Jean-Claude Van Damme. She lives in the Sonoran Desert of Arizona. Please visit her Web site at http://www.katherinelawrence.com.

Photo Credits

Cover © Ingrid Van Den Berg/Earth Scenes; pp. 1, 3, © Park, A. Surv. OSF/Earth Scenes; pp. 4–5 © David Muench/Corbis; p. 6 © D. Almany and E. Vicensy/Corbis; pp. 8–9, 24,–25, 36 © Anthony Bannister/Earth Scenes; p. 10 © Montheath/Animals Animals; p. 12 © Mark A. Chappell/Animals Animals; p. 15 © Dominique Brand/Animals Animals; p. 16 © Doug Wechsler/Earth Scenes; p. 18 © John Gerlach/Earth Scenes; p. 19 © Paul Freed/Earth Scenes; pp. 20, 23 © Joe McDonald/Animals Animals; p. 26 © David Smauel Robbins/Corbis; p. 27 © Valla, D.–Surviv OSF/Animals Animals; p. 29 © Dean Conger/Corbis; p. 30 © Austin J. Stevens/ Earth Scenes; p. 32 © Richard Shiell/ Earth Scenes; p. 34 © Stephen Ingram/Earth Scenes; p. 35 © Manfred Gottschalk/Earth Scenes; p. 40 © Ludovic Maisant/Corbis; pp. 42, 43 © AP/Wide World Photos; p. 47 © Sally A. Morgan/Ecoscene/Corbis; p. 48 © Andrew Bannister/Gallo Images/Corbis.

Designer: Thomas Forget; Editor: Annie Sommers;
Photo Researcher: Adriana Skura